Connect
with
Text

What is a
Poem?

Charlotte Guillain

raintree

Raintree is an imprint of Capstone Global Library Limited, a company incorporated in England and Wales having its registered office at 7 Pilgrim Street, London, EC4V 6LB – Registered company number: 6695582

www.raintree.co.uk
myorders@raintree.co.uk

Edited by Clare Lewis and Holly Beaumont
Designed by Philippa Jenkins
Picture research by Wanda Winch
Originated by Capstone Global Library Ltd
Produced by Helen McCreath
Printed and Bound at CTPS

ISBN 978 1 406 29005 9 (hardback)
18 17 16 15 14
10 9 8 7 6 5 4 3 2 1

ISBN 978 1 406 29010 3 (paperback)
19 18 17 16
10 9 8 7 6 5 4 3 2 1

British Library Cataloguing in Publication Data
A full catalogue record for this book is available from the British Library.

Acknowledgements
We would like to thank the following for permission to reproduce photographs: Capstone Studio: Karon Dubke, 4, 5, 10, 15, 16, 17, 26, 27, Charles Barnett III and Phil Miller, 21, Daniel Ferran, 11, DC Comics, 8, Dennis Calero, 20, Erik Lervold, 14, Gerardo Sandoval, 7, Jose Alfonso Ocampo Ruiz, 9, Peter McDonnell, 25, Richard Dominguez and Charles Barnett III, 24; Corbis: Reuters/Benoit Tessier, 22; Getty Images Inc: Gamma-Rapho/Marc Gantier, 19, Mark G. Renders, 18, SFX Magazine/Rob Monk, 12; Newscom: SIPA/ Saez Pascal, 6; Rex USA: c.Goldwyn/Everett, 13; Shutterstock: deedl, 23, solarseven, cover (bottom right), urfin, pencil

Disclaimer
All the internet addresses (URLs) given in this book were valid at the time of going to press. However, due to the dynamic nature of the internet, some addresses may have changed, or sites may have changed or ceased to exist since publication. While the author and publishers regret any inconvenience this may cause readers, no responsibility for any such changes can be accepted by either the author or the publishers.

Contents

Some words are shown in bold, **like this**. You can find out what they mean by looking in the glossary.

What do you like to read?

How often do you read poetry? Have you ever tried writing it? Most people don't read poems as much as other types of texts, such as novels or comics. It's easy to think that all poetry is difficult or old fashioned, but this is definitely not true. Poets have written all sorts of poems over the centuries.

Some poems are hilariously funny, some tell a story, while others show us something beautiful or important. Poems are also great to listen to. Not only can a poem paint pictures in your head, but the sounds that the words make can also affect the listener. Poetry can be very powerful!

What kind of text do you most enjoy reading?

Reading poems out loud can be fun for both you and your audience.

See for yourself

Ask a parent, teacher or librarian to show you one of their favourite poems. Ask them why they like it. What do you think of the poem? Would you like to read more poetry by this poet?

What is a poem?

A poem is a piece of text that has been written in a particular way. You'll notice the following things about poems:

- They are written so that the sound and the meaning of the words make the reader feel and think in certain ways. A poem often appeals to all of the reader's or listener's senses.

- Poems can be long or short. They can tell a story or just create a mood.

- A poem uses **rhythm** in special ways to have an effect on the reader. For example, a gentle, flowing rhythm might make the reader feel calm and relaxed.

- Some poems involve **rhyme**. This means that words at the end of some lines have similar sounds. Other poems don't rhyme.

- Some poems have very fixed structures. These can involve a set number of lines or the rhythm of each line. Other poems have no rules at all!

Popular poems

William Shakespeare is one of the most famous writers in the English language. Shakespeare is best known for his plays, but he also wrote poems. The most famous of these are the 154 **sonnets** he wrote about subjects like love and death. Sonnets have a special structure and most have 14 lines.

Poetry can range from works by Shakespeare to the **lyrics** of a pop song.

What is rhythm?

Rhythm is very important in poetry. The rhythm makes a poem sound very different to **prose**, which is the type of language used in most novels and short stories. When you hear a poem or listen to a song, there is a pattern of sound that is repeated. This regular beat is called the rhythm.

The rhythm can make the poem flow well, or it can have a jerky, awkward effect that can make the reader feel the way the poet wants them to. Some poems have a rhythm that sounds like the subject of the poem, for example a poem about a train might sound like an engine clattering along a track.

When you read a poem, see if you can clap out its rhythm with your hands.

SEE FOR YOURSELF

Open up a book of poetry and choose a poem to read aloud. How does the poem's rhythm make you feel?

Rap songs often have a very strong rhythm or beat.

9

What is a stanza?

Some poems are divided into **stanzas**. A stanza is a group of lines that are separated from other lines in the poem by a space. A stanza is sometimes called a verse. Different types of stanzas have different names, depending on the number of lines in them.

Popular poems

Shel Silverstein (1930–1999) was a US writer who wrote a lot of poetry for children. He wrote poems in couplets, such as *Ticklish Tom*, and many other poems with different structures. Find some of Silverstein's poems. What do you notice about the stanzas he has used?

Shel Silverstein was also a song writer and cartoonist.

A stanza that is made up of two lines is called a couplet. The lines of a couplet usually have the same **rhythm** and often they **rhyme**. One poem written in couplets is *maggie and milly and molly and may* by E.E. Cummings. Other poems can have stanzas with three lines, four lines or more.

The poem *The Tyger* by William Blake has stanzas with four lines.

Rhyming patterns

If you flick through a book of poetry and read the poems aloud, you'll notice that many of them **rhyme**. When a poem rhymes, some of the lines end with the same sound, for example "day" and "say".

When we look at the way rhyme works in a poem, we talk about the **rhyme scheme**. Poets can use different types of rhyme scheme in their work. Sometimes poetry is written in pairs of rhyming lines called **rhyming couplets**. For example:

I shot an arrow into the **air**
It fell to earth, I knew not **where**

(Henry Wadsworth Longfellow)

Poet Henry Wadsworth Longfellow used rhyming couplets in his poem *Paul Revere's Ride*.

Popular poems

The **lyrics**, or words, to many pop songs rhyme. The repeated sounds we hear in the song help to make the words stick in our minds. If you find yourself singing along to a song on the radio, listen carefully and see if it rhymes.

Some poems are written so the rhymes come in alternate lines, for example:

> I remember, I remember
> The house where I was **born**,
> The little window where the sun
> Came peeping in at **morn**.
>
> (Thomas Hood)

Other poems may have more complicated rhyme schemes.

The pop singer Adele has written many catchy songs.

Using sound in poems

Poets choosing the words for a poem think about how they can affect as many of a reader's or listener's senses as possible. Good poets use the sounds of the words in wonderful ways to make us think or feel different things.

Here are some of the sound effects poets use:

Effect	How it works	Example
alliteration	words in a poem start with the same consonant	**ghostly galleon** **wild whirling water**
assonance	words have vowel sounds in them that sound the same	**the mist swirled and curled around the house**
onomatopoeia	words sound like the thing they are describing	**"plop" sounds like the noise a stone makes when it plops into water**

Popular poems

Look for the poem *Cynthia in the Snow* by Gwendolyn Brooks. Read it out loud. Do you think the words "shushes" and "hushes" sound like the sound your feet make as you trudge through snow?

Can you find any examples of alliteration in this poem by Robert Frost?

MOWING

There was never a sound beside wood but one,
And that was my long scythe whispering to the
    ground.
What was it it whispered? I knew not well myself;
Perhaps it was something about the heat of the
    sun,
Something, perhaps about the lack of sound —
And that was why it whispered and did not speak.
It was no dream of the gift of idle hours,
Or easy gold at the hand of fay or elf:
Anything more than the truth would have seemed
    too weak.
To the earnest love that laid the swale in rows,
Not without feeble-pointed spikes of flowers
(Pale orchises), and scared a bright green snake.
The fact is the sweetest dream that labor knows,
My long scythe whispered and left the hay to
    make.

What is free verse?

Free verse is poetry that doesn't have any rules. Poems written in free verse don't have to be divided into **stanzas** or have a fixed **rhythm** or rhyming pattern. This type of poem can give poets a lot more freedom to express themselves in original ways.

When poets write free verse they still pick every word very carefully to have a powerful effect on the reader. As well as **alliteration**, **assonance** and **onomatopoeia**, poets may also use other effects, for example:

Effect	How it works	Example
	Compares one thing with another	as cold as ice fog like a blanket
	Describes something as being another thing	his heart is ice the fog was a blanket

Popular poems

In the poem *Fog*, the poet Carl Sandburg uses a metaphor to describe the fog as a cat walking around. When poets describe things as if they are animals or people it is called **personification**. Another example of this can be found in William Wordsworth's poem *Daffodils*, where he writes that the flowers are "tossing their heads in a sprightly dance".

You may sometimes write free verse at school.

Nursery rhymes

A nursery rhyme is a traditional poem or song that has been around for hundreds of years. Some nursery **rhymes** are lullabies, with gentle **rhythms** to send a tired baby to sleep. Others tell stories, such as *Mary Had a Little Lamb*. They often have very strong rhythms and rhymes that make them easy to remember, for example:

It's raining, it's pouring,
The old man is snoring.
He went to bed
And bumped his head
And couldn't get up in the morning.

SIMPLE SIMON

Simple Simon met a pieman
Going to the fair
Says Simple Simon to the pieman
Let me taste your ware

How many nursery rhymes do you know by heart? If you can't remember any, find a nursery rhyme book and see how many you recognize. What do you think helps us to remember these poems?

Many nursery rhymes include lots of repeated words or nonsense words. For example, in *Old MacDonald Had a Farm* the sounds "e-i-e-i-o" are repeated, as well as the animal noises. This makes the poem lots of fun to read or sing!

Some of the first poems we hear are nursery rhymes read to us by our parents.

Poems that tell a story

Many writers use a poem to tell a story. In the past, poets wrote epic poems that told long stories, often about heroes who go off on great adventures. Some examples are the ancient Greek epic poems *Iliad* and *Odyssey*, and the Old English poem *Beowulf*.

The writer Roald Dahl wrote lots of funny story poems.

Popular poems

The Victorian poet Alfred Tennyson wrote the poem *The Charge of the Light Brigade*. This poem describes what happens to a brigade of soldiers who ride bravely to fight a battle they have no hope of winning. It tells the story of a real-life event in a war when many soldiers died.

The English poet Alfred Tennyson lived from 1809–1892.

Ballads are another type of poem that tell a story. Many ballads were originally sung to an audience. One very famous ballad is Samuel Taylor Coleridge's *The Rime of the Ancient Mariner*. This is the story of a ghostly sailor and his tale of a disastrous voyage.

Today many poets tell stories in their poems. These poems may have a narrator and a range of characters. The poet has to tell the story in fewer words than in a novel or short story, so the language they choose is very important.

Funny poems

Some of your favourite poems may be funny.
Writers have used poems to make people laugh for
thousands of years. Some funny poems have a fixed
structure. A **limerick**, for example, always has five
lines with the first, second and fifth line rhyming,
and a **rhyming couplet** on the third and fourth lines.
Here is an example of a limerick by Edward Lear:

There was a Young Lady whose chin
Resembled the point of a pin;
So she had it made sharp,
And purchased a harp,
And played several tunes with her chin.

Popular poems

Many modern children's
poets write funny poems.
Jack Prelutsky is an
American poet who has
written lots of famous
funny poems, such as *I
Made a Noise at School This
Morning* and *Jellyfish Stew*.

Jack Prelutsky is a singer
as well as a poet and often
sets his poems to music.

Michael Rosen is a British poet who writes and performs hilarious poems like *Chocolate Cake* and *The Itch*.

Edward Lear also wrote nonsense poems, such as *The Owl and the Pussycat*. Another poet, Hilaire Belloc, was well known for his ***Cautionary Tales***. These poems tell the stories of children who have bad habits, or don't listen to adults and meet a sticky end. For example, a boy called Jim runs off at the zoo and is eaten by a lion!

Poems with patterns

Some poems need to be read off the page because of the shapes and patterns they make. An **acrostic poem** is usually written so that if you read the first letter of each word downwards, they spell out a new message or word. A list poem often repeats the same words at the start of each line. List poems often list lots of different information about something.

Popular poems

A **haiku** is a type of poem that was originally written in Japan. Haikus only have three lines. The first line has five **syllables**, the second line has seven syllables and the last line has five syllables. Haikus describe a mood. Here is an example:

> Blowing from the west
> All the fallen leaves gather
> In the dark forest.

Jackie Kay's poem *Waves* is a list poem that can also be written out to look like waves on the sea.

Other poems may be written so that the lines make a shape or a picture that is linked to the meaning of the words. Sometimes these are called **calligrams**. The poet Gina Douthwaite has written many poems that make amazing shapes on the page, such as *Sweet Tooth*, and also *Do Not Disturb the Dinosaur*, where the whole poem is shaped like a dinosaur!

Performance poetry

Some poets write performance poetry. These poems are specially written to be read out loud to an audience. When a performance poet performs their work it is a bit like hearing music being performed. The poet is able to communicate directly with the audience and add to the effects of the language with the way they speak and move on the stage.

Linton Kwesi Johnson was born in Jamaica. He performs his poetry with Jamaican reggae music, which suits his style of verse.

The American poet Marc Smith invented the poetry slam.

Many performance poets want to communicate a message they feel strongly about, such as politics or the environment. They can reach people who would not normally pick up a book of poetry. Lots of new poets perform at **poetry slams**. This is when lots of poets read their work out loud and are judged by members of the audience. This can be very exciting for the poets and for the audience!

Write your own

Why not try writing your own poem to be performed to an audience? Think about something you care about. What do you want to tell people? Write a short poem and then perform it for your family and friends. Make sure you get their feedback.

Take it further...

Start by picking up an **anthology** of poems written by different poets and flick through to see what appeals to you. If you find a poem you like, look out for more information about the poet and their work. What do you notice about each poem? Is it funny or does it tell a story? Can you spot any way the poet uses language to have an effect on you, for example, **onomatopoeia** or **alliteration**? When you've found some poems you like, try reading them out loud with your friends and family.

Allan Ahlberg has written many poems about life at school and other childhood experiences.

If you want more ideas to help you find poetry that appeals to you, you could try asking your teacher or a librarian. You might want to go to a poetry performance or slam and hear poetry being read. And of course, you could try writing your own!

Ideas to get you started

Try writing a list poem about what you do on each day of the week. Try to include some alliteration if you can!

"On Monday I...
On Tuesday I..."

Try writing a **limerick** that starts with this line:

"There once was a girl called Marie..."

Write a poem that explains to your teacher why you haven't done your homework.

Glossary

acrostic poem   poem where the first letters of each word spell another word down the page

alliteration   when words start with the same consonant

anthology   collection of poems, often by different poets, in one book

assonance   when words have vowel sounds in them that sound the same

calligram   poem that makes a picture when written down

cautionary tale   poem or story that warns against bad habits or behaviour

haiku   short poem, originally from Japan

limerick   funny poem with a particular structure

lyrics   words to a song

metaphor   when something is described as being another thing

onomatopoeia   when words sound like the thing they are describing

personification   when something is described as if it is a person

poetry slam   competition where poets perform their work and are judged by an audience

prose   writing that isn't poetry

rhyme   when words have the same sounds

rhyme scheme   way in which the lines of a poem rhyme

rhyming couplet   pair of lines in a poem that rhyme

rhythm   beat

simile   when one thing is compared with another

sonnet   poem with 14 lines

stanza   verse of a poem

syllable   one sound within a word

Find out more

Books

101 Poems for Children, Carol Ann Duffy (Macmillan, 2013)

How to Write Poems, Wes Magee (QED, 2008)

Off By Heart: Poems for Children to Learn and Remember, Roger Stevens (A&C Black, 2013)

Pizza, Pigs and Poetry, Jack Prelutsky (Greenwillow Books, 2008)

Websites

www.poetry4kids.com
Read lots of poems and tips on how to write your own poetry on this website.

www.poetryarchive.org/childrensarchive/home.do
Listen to some great poetry being read on this website.

http://poetryzone.co.uk
Get your own poetry put on this website for other people to read.

www.michaelrosen.co.uk/poems.html
Read some of Michael Rosen's poems here.

Index